Australian Shepherds

*A Practical Guide To Understanding & Caring For
Your Australian Shepherd*

Bowe Packer

TABLE OF CONTENTS

PUBLISHERS NOTES

Disclaimer

This publication is intended to provide helpful and informative material. It is in no way intended to cover every aspect of raising and caring for Australian Shepherds.

With that said, please understand the author has made every attempt to provided quality information at a good price.

The author and publisher specifically disclaim all responsibility for any liability, loss or risk, personal or otherwise, which is incurred as a consequence, directly or indirectly, from the use or application of any contents of this book.

Any and all product names referenced within this book are the trademarks of their respective owners. None of these owners have sponsored, authorized, endorsed, or approved this book.

Always read all information provided by the manufacturers' product labels before using their products. The author and publisher are not responsible for claims made by manufacturers.

Paperback Edition 2014

Manufactured in the United States of America

DEDICATION

I dedicate this book to all those people out there who remind us of the things we have forgotten about ourselves.

And this holds especially true of my beautiful and amazing wife, Alma. She is the one woman who has the most amazing talent to let me grow and love the things about myself that I have not fully accepted.

I cherish the love she has for me when I may not know how to love myself.

May we all have this kind of beautiful soul in our life.

Sent from LOVE,

Sunshine In My Soul

INTRODUCTION

Do you know the top three reasons that people get a dog for themselves or their family? For most people it is the loyalty, companionship and unconditional love that dogs provide that you simply can't find anywhere else. After all, how many times do you see regular people doing things for others simply because it makes someone else happy without any regard for themselves? Unfortunately it doesn't happen nearly as much as we would like to think it does.

Australian Shepherds on the other hand are able to provide those three things in abundance. They are loving, loyal, and above all, they don't care what you do, they just want to be loved in return. If you're looking for a beautiful, friendly and happy addition to your family (no matter how big or how small) then you'll definitely want to think about getting an Australian Shepherd.

This type of dog wasn't bred to just laze around on your floor and take up space. It was actually bred to be a work dog. These dogs were originally intended to work on farms typically herding sheep or cattle which means that your new Australian Shepherd (Aussie for short) may have a tendency of herding your family, children or other pets.

WHAT TO KNOW

This book is going to tell you everything you need to understand to determine whether or not an Aussie is the right dog for you. If you've already got an Aussie then this book will tell you everything you've ever wanted to know about your dog. We'll discuss some facts about you and your lifestyle to determine if this type of dog is going to be the best choice for you because these dogs are very active and definitely want attention.

Think about what you are capable of doing. If you aren't capable of giving a dog plenty of exercise and attention then this is not the dog for you. If you aren't ready to do the research required then you might want to wait to get a dog altogether. But if you think you're ready for the responsibility and the treasure of owning your own dog then let's get started finding out if an Aussie is the perfect choice for you.

So You Want An Aussie

All right, so you've decided that you want to get an Aussie for your family. You're going to learn all about the things you'll need to do so that your family is ready for the big commitment of having this happy (and large) dog in your household. You'll learn everything from puppy-proofing your home to feeding and grooming your new pet. You'll also learn all about the best ways to get your puppy physically active.

You'll learn plenty about these dogs in general as well such as where they came from (here's a hint, it wasn't 'The Land Down Under') and where the name originated as well. So let's get started finding out more about these amazing dogs and what you can expect when you welcome one into your life.

Chapter 1 - Where Does He Come From?

When you think of an Australian Shepherd where do you think he comes from? Chances are you think of him as being from Australia right? It sounds like the right answer since the word is right there in his name. The truth of the matter however, is that this hardworking dog is not originally from Australia at all. This dog is from somewhere entirely different.

Dogs as Part of the Family

Back in the day everyone in a family was expected to work hard. No matter how old you were it was expected that you would do your part and you would take your turn at the wheel. Even little children could be helpers in small ways such as washing dishes or sweeping floors. Even the dogs were expected to help and that's why many dogs were bred for helping with livestock.

Australian Shepherds were one of those types of dogs. They are actually excellent at herding smaller animals and this made them nearly invaluable on farms. But of course it takes time to breed a quality animal that is capable of herding other animals without hurting them. So where did that all begin?

Europeans came over to settle America and brought their pets along with them. Now pets were a working part of the family remember so these were working dogs. Some dogs were herders while others may have been guard dogs. The dogs that were brought over varied from English Shepherds to Welsh Grey Sheepdogs. But dogs generally don't stay purebred for long. Much as America became the melting pot of different races and cultures mixing together so too did dog breeds.

WESTWARD HO!

Most of the people who originally came to America would settle in the East simply because that was the closest place they landed on. So for the longest time everyone lived on the East coast where the land was cooler and the dogs and people were accustomed to those moderate climates. It was much like the land that they had left in many respects and there was no need to make a lot of changes to the animals they used to protect their livestock.

The western part of the country was extremely hot, something that most Europeans knew little about. This area was arid and could be very difficult for anyone traveling there. In the northwest however, weather could be extremely cold, far colder than what the Europeans were accustomed to. The only people in the far south were the Spanish and their own dogs. However things began to change with the Gold Rush of 1849.

When people began traveling further and further to the west they had to bring their sheep with them. Those sheep began to reproduce at extreme rates. But people wanted more and more. So those people brought sheep from Australia.

INCREASE IN HERDING DOGS

Dogs were bred differently to survive the storms and strange temperatures that occurred in the west. The dogs weren't capable of continuing their jobs in those temperatures. So the dogs needed to be bred properly. They needed to be fast and they needed to respond to orders as well. A dog to fit all of these requirements was not easy to come by. But what came about was a big dog with the ability to do everything necessary. The dogs became known as Australian Shepherds though this name had nothing to do with where they came from.

BECOMING FRIENDS

There is no one currently alive that knows where the name 'Australian Shepherd' actually came from. There are theories of course such as the fact that these dogs did, in fact, come from Australia with the Basque sheepherders. However the truth of the matter is that Basque sheepherders came from Europe or Latin America in the 19th century when the Australian Shepherd was first bred.

Australian sheepdogs were similar in many ways to the current 'Australian Shepherd' however they were not exactly the same. They weren't as agile and yet they were similar colors to the dogs that we know today.

GHOST-EYES

It's believed that the markings on these dogs were what caused the new breeds to be called Australian Shepherds themselves even though they weren't from Australia. Both dogs shared this coloring though little else.

Native Americans thought the ghost eyed dogs were sacred because of that eye color. They refused to interact with anyone who even owned the dog let along the dogs themselves. They were considered more than just dogs and almost like gods.

Over time the dogs were needed and they were bred for that purpose. They were agile, versatile, strong, obedient and smart. They were able to do anything that was asked of them and they could do it quickly. They were a brand new breed but they weren't truly known as such. In fact, they were thought of as simply a small strain and barely anyone knew of their existence for a long time to come.

Jay Sisler-Australian Shepherd Wrangler

Though not everyone may know who Jay Sisler is, if you're an Aussie fan then chances are you do. He began in the 1950's training dogs to perform tricks at rodeos and his favorite was, by far, the Aussie because of its ability to learn quickly and retain that information.

Later these dogs were cast in to classic Disney movies, *Run Appaloosa Run* and *Stub: The Greatest Cowdog in the West*. These films helped to pave the way for greater knowledge and love for the Aussie as its own breed. People began to see them everyone and they began to want one for themselves as well. So thanks to Jay Sisler, these dogs are now well known and well loved.

The Australian Shepherd Club of America

In 1957 this club was created for those who already loved this dog. There weren't a lot of people in the club but when knowledge about it spread, so did love for the Australian Shepherd. It took only a few more years, until 1971, before the dogs received more support to achieve competitive status and it was six more years before they were considered a true breed.

Of course the American Kennel Club was the last step to the dog officially being declared its own breed. Without their support it simply wouldn't happen. However it was the breeders that negated this step. They were afraid that Australian Shepherds would be considered two different classes of dogs, herding/working animals and show dogs. In the year 1985 the breeders declined to approach the AKC with a proposal of breed recognition.

A new club was formed, The United States Australian Shepherd Association petitioned for recognition of the dogs instead and the request was granted in the year 1993. This dog is now capable of competing at all AKC dog shows and actually has proven to be a very strong competitor there.

The Australian Shepherd is considered an excellent dog and is loved by many yet it is not for everyone. If you want to find out if your home is a good place to raise an Australian Shepherd then look over the next chapter of this book.

CHAPTER 2- IS AN AUSSIE RIGHT FOR YOU?

Dogs require a lot of time and work. Some require even more time and work than others. So how do you determine if you're ready for the responsibility of a dog? Well it's not necessarily going to be easy. You're going to need to think about your family, your home, your lifestyle and the type of dog you're thinking about getting. Specifically, we're going to talk about your likelihood of meshing well with an Australian Shepherd.

NEED TO WORK

An Aussie needs to do work. The love doing just that. So if you are going to get an Aussie you want to make sure that they aren't just sitting around the house because they don't appreciate being regular pets. These dogs will get into some kind of trouble if you don't have a job for them to do. These are working dogs and that's really all the want, that and a loving home.

No matter what's around an Australian Shepherd will find some way to herd. This is their best trait and they will herd anything that moves whether it's children, ducks, sheep or other dogs. You'll likely be surprised all the times your dog starts herding others and trying to keep tabs on your family. These dogs will do anything from bringing in the paper to helping with therapy.

Now remember also that your Australian Shepherd wants to be the Alpha of your household. Your dog wants to be in charge so make sure that you're letting him have the reins at least once in a while and make sure you don't have too many big, bossy dogs in one place.

WHAT TO KNOW

Remember that the first step for your dog is going to be achieving Alpha status. So whoever is the current dominant of your party, whether that's you or another dog. You will want to make sure that you're still maintaining enough status in the household. If you let your Australian Shepherd take over your household you'll have even more problems in the long run. So stay the top dog.

TRAIN HIM RIGHT

An Australian Shepherd must be trained properly in order to succeed. You want to make sure they learn self-control and also that you are gaining dominance. If your dog is too overbearing you'll be causing more problems in your home. Make sure your dog is prepared throughout its entire life from childhood through adulthood.

PROPER EXERCISE IS KEY

Your Aussie needs to get proper exercise. It needs to work very hard however and can't simply walk through a park. You need to make sure that you're playing vigorous games with your Aussie or you'll end up with a very unhappy pup. You're also going to want to be an energetic person yourself. Whether you have a skill with jogging or enjoy camping you'll be able to get along with your Aussie much better.

If you have the ability to spend plenty of time with your pet then you're better off still. You want to make sure that you are spending plenty of time getting exercise for your Aussie and then you want to make sure you're spending more time with your dog even after the exercise portion of your time is done. You're going to need plenty of socialization for your pet after you're done getting all that work done. You won't be able to get rid of your puppy when you return home because they will be glued to you all the time. Remember that without the right level of socialization your puppy may end up barking, growling or even biting at strangers because of this lack socialization.

SPLIT PERSONALITY

The temperament of Australian Shepherds can be difficult to pin down. Some of these dogs are perfect for spending time out in the field and can work harder than others. They will also be very busy and want to be doing things even more than ever. They tend to be distinguishable because they are smaller than other Australian Shepherds and they are also much sharper in temperament.

The more mellow of Australian Shepherds tend to be better for spending time with a family. If you want to have a pet then this is the dog to choose. It is still going to want plenty of attention and plenty of exercise. That's just the way this breed of dog operates.

GROOMING NEEDS

These types of dogs have what is known as a double coat. This means that the topcoat as well as the undercoat need to be brushed continuously. If you aren't careful they'll shed way more than other dogs and they'll definitely be providing you with plenty of work both with grooming and other things.

MAKING A COMMITMENT

When you take in a puppy you're going to be making a long term commitment. Dogs live for approximately 15 years depending on the type of dog. An Australian Shepherd could live this long easily and you'll need to have the ability and the willingness to take care of them for that entire length of time.

Remember that all animals have the potential for health problems and Australian Shepherds are definitely no exception. These could have spinal defects, eye problems and even potential hearing problems. All of these things seem to relate to pigmentation problems within the breed itself.

Hip Dysplasia

One of the most common problems that affects this breed of dog is hip dysplasia. This disease causes severe problems that lead to deterioration and arthritis in the dogs. What happens is the hip joint grows in an improper manner causing problems throughout the hip. Though more common in male dogs this disorder can definitely occur in females as well and tends to be genetic.

Consider it All

Once you've read through all of this if you're still sure that an Australian Shepherd is the best option for you then check out this website: http://dogtime.com/matchup/answer to decide if this is the proper dog for you. If you still think this is the right dog for you then you want to make sure you keep reading to learn more about the Aussie's available for you.

CHAPTER 3- PICKING THE PERFECT AUSSIE PUP?

Okay so now you're all ready to get an Australian Shepherd for yourself. The first step is making this decision. But you're going to need to make some other decisions as well. You need to find out more about these dogs and also far more about your family and what you have the ability to take care of. You have another step to follow now which starts with two different parts. You want to find a dog that really fits in with your family.

If you are planning to get a purebred puppy then you want to make sure that you're getting all the proper papers necessary to prove its purebred status. You want to make sure all the paperwork is correct and accurate and then you'll be able to add to your family quickly, easily and happily as well. This is when you'll get to choose the right puppy for you and your desires.

You'll be able to find breeders of Australian Shepherds quickly and easily. You'll be able to use the internet to locate all different places where Australian Shepherds can be found.

CHECK THE SHOWS

A dog show can be a great place to find Australian Shepherd breeders. You'll be able to talk to people who have these dogs for themselves and find out more about where they came from and also tips to help in raising your own Australian Shepherd. You'll be able to learn more than you ever thought you needed to know and you'll be able to get more information about these dogs so you can better understand what you'll need to raise one.

PROPER ETHICS

Ethics can be very important. You'll want to find a dog breeder that has proper ethics because they will have a way of putting you at ease. You won't have to worry about anything because the breeder will feel comfortable talking with you about their puppies and they will be sure they aren't ill in any way. If you're comfortable with the person you're getting your dog from then you are more likely to be getting a good dog.

Make sure you have questions and make sure they have questions for you as well. If they don't have any questions then they aren't as considerate of their pets. The conscientious and ethical breeder will want to ensure that their puppies are being taken in by people who truly will love them and care for them as well.

What Type of Dog

Now you'll remember we talked about there being two different types of Australian Shepherds. These dogs can be either show dogs or they can be regular pets. If you find the right breeder they're going to ask you which of these two things you really want your dog for. That's because there's a slight difference between the dogs and you'll only make them and yourself miserable if you get the wrong one.

Breed standards really only matter when you're selecting a dog for showing. A dog that is meant to be a family pet simply needs to be healthy and small 'imperfections' in the coat or coloring or anything else simply won't matter as much. You also won't care too much about the breeding because you won't be breeding the dog or entering it in shows where that kind of thing will matter.

If you want to show your dog then you're definitely going to need to look into proper breeding. You want to make sure that your dog has papers that display his background and that he has no imperfections that will get him disqualified from regular competitions. Any of these things could be detrimental to your end goals and dogs that don't fit the right criteria are not destined for show.

You'll want to remember of course that there is no way to predict whether a dog, no matter how perfect it may appear, is going to be a winner in shows. You'll only be able to determine whether the dog has the potential to be a winner or not based on look, health and breeding.

Don't Forget to Ask

Meeting a breeder is very important for a lot of reasons. If you're looking to get an Australian Shepherd you want to be sure that your dog is going to fit a certain level of qualifications. You want to make sure you really understand the puppy you're getting and where it came from. Make sure you ask the right questions so you don't end up blindsided later on.

1. Do you have the papers?

You want to see papers for any dog that is claimed to be purebred. If you don't have papers then you can't claim the dog as a pure Australian Shepherd. You want to make sure that you know where the dog has come from and where it's parents came from. In fact you want at least three to five generations of healthy Australian Shepherd ancestors for any purebred dog you purchase.

Next you want to make sure that you are weighing out those papers. Just because ancestors of this dog were winners doesn't mean these puppies will be just like the fact that it was bred by common pets won't be a precursor to the dog being only good for being a pet. You will only have an idea of the lineage and not one of what the dog is capable of.

2. What the pregnancy planned?

Just like with people a planned pregnancy can tell you a lot more about the puppy. You'll be able to tell that if the pregnancy was planned the other dog was more than likely an Australian Shepherd. On the other hand if the pregnancy was not planned you won't have any way of knowing what the breed of the dog really is.

3. Why was the sire chosen?

The sire of a dog is the father, the male that was chosen to impregnate the female dog. If a breeder breeds their dog then they chose the two dogs specifically for a very important reason. You want to make sure that you are getting all the information to find out why that specific dog was chosen. Does it have a good history? Has it produced winners in the past? Was it a winner? All of these things will help you learn more about the puppy.

4. What faults do the parents have?

Find out what the mother and father both do that isn't as good. You'll want to make sure that the breeder you talk to has at least one fault for each of the dogs because this means they are a good breeder and they are upfront about their dogs. They will also let you know some good qualities at the same time.

5. Why did you breed the dogs?

If the breeder is simply trying to make money then you aren't looking for their dogs. You want a breeder who is doing it simply to extend the species because they love the dogs. Making money should only be a bonus to helping the dogs themselves. Breeders who love what they do are more likely to take care of the dogs they are training and caring for.

THE BACKUP PLAN

Make sure that you check out more than one breeder. You may find one that you think is a great choice but turns out not to be. When you visit more than one breeder you can get a better idea of what is normal and what isn't. You'll also be able to weigh out the pros and cons of each breeder and the puppies they have to offer and decide which is going to be the best option for you. Remember of course that you will want to make sure that you get on the list (there will likely be a wait list if the pups aren't born yet).

Even if the pups are born there could be a waitlist for purebred puppies so make sure you get put on it quickly and make sure you respond immediately if you get a call that a puppy is available. Most breeders will hold them for a certain amount of time however the people further down the list want to know right away if you aren't going to take the puppy that's being held for you.

Even though it can be annoying a waitlist is actually a good thing. This means that the breeder you've selected is known and that they produce quality pups.

When You Just Can't Wait

If you're tired of waiting around for your first choice breeder you can get on the list for your second choice instead. This breeder may have a shorter list or they may be able to give you a pup right away. Just make sure that you aren't taking the puppy too soon. They can often be seen close to the sixth week after birth however they should not be separated from their mother or dam until they are at least eight weeks old.

Socializing Properly

Socializing is a crucial step for your puppy. You want to make sure that they are getting the attention that they need and that they are learning how to interact with others. The best way to do this is to spend time with them. The breeder should be socializing their puppies from the time they are born however the first time you get to go see them you'll want to make sure you're spending at least half an hour playing with the puppy yourself. This will give you enough time to really experience the dogs themselves and it will allow you to find out more about their temperament and fit with your family.

If you dog is going to become a part of your family then it is very important to take the family with you to see it. The breeders know that most of their potential customers are going to bring a family and they expect you all to get down with the dogs and get to know them better to make a good choice for your entire family.

SPENDING TIME

You want to make sure you're spending time with the entire litter and not selecting just one puppy right off the bat. Playing with all of the dogs will help you to better understand their personalities and the way that they will fit in with your own family. You don't want a puppy that is too dominating and you don't want one that is too submissive either. You want to get one that has the right balance of play. You also want to get firsthand experience of this. Don't be afraid to get down on the floor with the puppies and see what they do. A good puppy should run right over and greet you. When you pick them up they shouldn't have any problem being held.

When you're holding the puppy touch their paws, mouth and ears. If the puppy is properly socialized it will have no problem with this. If not then you don't want that puppy. Try the same with at least a couple of the dog's siblings and then think about the way they all act. Are they friendly around strangers? Do they get startled easily? These answers will help you determine if this is the right type of puppy for you.

CHECK THEM OUT ALONE

You're going to want to spend time with each individual puppy as well to get a better idea of how they act by themselves. Just like you are probably different around your friends or your family a dog will act differently by itself as well. You want to know the individual puppy's temperament and this is the only way to truly do this.

Different tests will help you to measure the puppy that you are thinking about choosing. The Ultimate Puppy Aptitude Test is one of those methods. In this way you'll be able to learn more about the dog itself from its personality and behavior to its curiosity level. It's also generally seen as a way of predicting what the dog will be like in the future when it's grown.

The aptitude test requires you to measure how well the puppy interacts with other people. You want one that is going to be comfortable around people. A dog that is fearful or aggressive around everyone is not the type of dog you want around your family. You'll always be wondering what the dog could do at any moment?

CAUTION VS. CURIOSITY

You want a dog that has some curiosity and that likes to check things out but you don't want it to be so curious it simply throws caution to the wind and does whatever it wants. You want to be sure that your puppy knows how to properly react to any situation that it may find itself in and that could be a difficult thing to test.

What you're going to need are:

- Keys
- Squeaky toy
- Umbrella
- Towel
- Six foot rope
- Treats
- Stopwatch

You're going to me measuring several different things about your potential new puppy including:

- Desire to be with people
- Curiosity about something new
- Extroverted vs. introverted
- Reaction and recovery
- Desire to work with people
- Reaction to handling and restraint
- Prey drive
- Trainability
- Physical activity level

What you want to do is rate the way the puppy responds to different situations with a one, two or three score. A one is extreme reactions and this is not something that you want. Two is a moderate reaction and three is the perfect answer. We're even going to tell you exactly what should happen to give the puppy each score.

TEST #1: ACTIVITY AND CURIOSITY LEVEL

Place the puppy in the middle of the "testing area." Watch him for two minutes. When the puppy approaches you, be still and just ignore him. (Yes, it will be difficult!)

Give him a one (1) if he doesn't move around or explore his environment. Also, give a one if he avoids you. Running and jumping however are also a one.

A moderate score of two (2) means he remains still for a few moments, then only slowly begins to investigate. Give him the same score if he's cautious about meeting you or sniffing objects around him.

A top score means the dog is moving around with confidence, sniffing at things and interacting appropriately. He will also interact with you calmly and confidently.

TEST #2: SOCIAL ATTRACTION

In this test, move at least 10 feet away from the dog after you set him on the floor. Now try to call him over to you. You can clap, yell or whatever you want to try and get him to come to you.

Score him low (1) if he ignores you, tries to hide, or starts to approach you and then turns, trying to get out of the area.

You'll give him a moderate score of two (2) if he approaches you gradually and cautiously.

And give him a high score of three (3) if he responds quickly to you and "happily" runs up to you, with his tail wagging enthusiastically.

TEST #3: FOLLOWING

Quickly move away from the pup, calling and encouraging him to come with you. Keep moving for about a 10-foot length.

If he runs the other way he gets a one (1). If he acts aggressively then he also gets a one.

Give him a moderate score of two (2) if he moves towards you but remains back. He may appear cautious.

The highest score goes to the dog that follows enthusiastically and trustingly.

TEST #4: RESTRAINT

Sit down on the floor and hold the puppy for approximately 30 seconds. Try to keep him from moving by holding him around the chest close to you.

A one (1) means the dog tried to get away, struggled, scratched, trembled or bit at you. You'll want to let him go if he panics too much and most definitely if he tries to bite at you.

A (2) means that the dog struggled somewhat but then seemed to relax the longer you held him.

Finally a three (3) means the dog relaxed as soon as you grabbed them and didn't have any trouble with you holding him as long as you wanted.

TEST #5: HANDLING

Next try sitting down and petting the puppy from the head and ears all the way down to the feet and tail. You should be talking in a soothing and calm voice the entire time. There are several ways the puppy could respond to this type of attention.

A one (1) means the dog tried to bite or get away from you and your attention.

A two (2) means the dog resists at first and then relaxes and enjoys the attention.

Finally if the dog relaxes immediately then it scores a three (3).

TEST #6: SOUND SENSITIVITY

Now you're going to test how the dog responds to new sounds and surprises. Drop your keys a couple feet behind the dog and see what he does. He should react in certain ways to the initial surprise.

If the dog is startled or frightened or even if he attacks the keys then he gets a low score.

A moderate score is achieved if the dog is startled yet manages to recover within 20 seconds but not less than 10.

A high score is achieved if the dog manages to recover from the initial shock after only ten seconds or less and then wanders over to check out the situation.

TEST #7: SIGHT SENSITIVITY

This is when you want to check the way that the dog responds to visual stimulation. Tie the string around the towel and pull it across the floor in front of the puppy. If the puppy moves then you stop. Let the towel sit on the floor and wait to see the reaction.

A one (1) is awarded if the dog ignores the towel or runs away from it. Give this score also if the puppy tries to attack the towel in an angry or aggressive manner.

If the puppy moves toward the towel while it moves but ignores it when it stops then give them a moderate score.

Finally if the dog attempts to playfully chase the towel and even pounce at it whether it's moving or not then give them a high score.

TEST #8: FETCH

Take out the squeaky toy and show it to the puppy to get their attention. When you have their attention throw the ball and try and get them to fetch it. Monitor what they do next.

If the puppy ignores the object or appears frightened then they get a one (1).

If the puppy moves towards it but then decides to ignore it or reaches it but does not respond then give them a medium score. This is a two (2).

Finally give the puppy a three (3) if they chase down the toy and even pick it up. They may even attempt to bring the toy back to you for a real game of fetch.

TEST #9: REACTION TO SURPRISE

Take out an umbrella six feet from the puppy and open it before setting it on the floor. Don't make any gesture or call towards the puppy, simply step back and watch what happens next.

If the puppy seems afraid or attacks the umbrella then he is awarded a one (1).

If the puppy manages to approach the umbrella cautiously or is startled but recovers within 20 seconds give them a moderate score as well.

Finally if the puppy shows high levels of interest in the umbrella or is startled but recovers within 10 seconds give him a high score.

TEST #10: TRAINABILITY

The final test uses the treats we mentioned earlier. You're going to hold out several of the treats and simply give them to the puppy so they understand what the treats are and that they want one. You'll next try and hold the treat slightly above the dog's head so it has to bring its front paws off the floor.

The dog will score a one if they seem uninterested in the treat or your actions or if they move away.

A moderate score is awarded if the puppy initially is interested in the treat but then seems to lose interest by becoming distracted.

Finally if the puppy follows the treat with their eyes and their body as you move it then they receive a three.

Now add up the points and see what you have.

10-14 is the lowest scores you could possibly get. These puppies aren't very good in any of the categories tested and they likely won't be a good companion for you and your family. They definitely won't be good at competitions.

15-19 are still low scores though not quite that good. This type of dog is going to take a lot of work simply to get to the level of being a good family pet. It will take a lot of effort on your part and you may not want to take on that kind of extreme commitment.

20-24 is an average score. These puppies need a little bit more work than what you may be looking for but it won't take too much effort to get them to the right level. This is still a job for a more experienced pet owner however.

25-30 is the highest level a dog can achieve on this test. These are the best choices for your family and for you. They are the dogs you definitely would like to add to your family as a pet or a show dog.

WHAT ABOUT A RESCUE?

Some people choose to adopt an Australian Shepherd rather than getting a puppy from a breeder. These adoptions are completed by breeders or rescue homes and tend to work with dogs that have been abandoned for whatever reason. The dogs are given to families who agree to foster them until a new home can be found. You'll have to make sure you're looking hard at these homes as there are a great many throughout the country where you can find a dog that would be a perfect addition to your family. In the meantime the foster family takes great care of them.

WHY TAKE A RESCUE?

One of the good things about taking in rescue dogs is the fact that you will get more information about the dog than if you adopt a puppy. A rescue dog is generally full grown and they have a family as well. They will be able to tell you what the dog is like and how it reacts with other dogs, cats, birds or even other people. When you adopt these dogs they are socialized and housebroken and may even be spayed or neutered. These individuals will also be able to tell you if the dog has any kind of health problems or needs special treatment so you can be prepared before you ever take it home.

WHY AVOID A RESCUE?

There are some bad things about rescue dogs however. One is that the dog may have been abused or maltreated by their original owner. As a result of this they may have developed some bad habits. They may not be as friendly as you would like. Another negative is that these dogs are usually halfway or fully grown and are very unlikely to be puppies. If you really want a puppy you're going to want to look elsewhere.

Forget "Your Way"

If you're looking for a very specific dog then know that you likely won't find that dog at a rescue. Specifics like eye color or fur coloring likely won't occur in a rescue dog unless you look for a very long time. You'll also be required to pay quite a bit for the adoption process through one of these shelters because the dog has already been checked over by a vet, spayed or neutered, and cared for for a long time.

This dog has likely also experienced some level of training and quite a bit of socialization as well. The dog is ready to join a family and the rescue workers need to get some of the money back they spent on that dog so they can take on another dog in its place. These people need the money because they are non-profit and anything they get from you can help more animals in the future.

CHAPTER 4- GETTING THE HOUSE READY FOR YOUR PUPPY

The next step is getting your home ready for your new puppy. You want to make sure the puppy is going to be safe and that your home is going to be safe as well. After all, you don't want your priceless treasures to become dog food and you don't want your precious puppy to get hurt by something falling on them. So do you remember baby-proofing your house? Because this is going to be a very similar endeavor.

THROUGH YOUR PUPPY'S EYES

Walk through your house before you bring your new puppy home. You want to think about everything the way your new puppy is going to think about it. Is that blanket hanging over the couch a new tug-of-war toy? Is the slightly ajar door to the basement a new place to explore? Anything that looks like your puppy would want to get into it should be examined. Is it safe for the puppy and for the item if your puppy decides to explore? If not then make sure the item is moved.

Getting rid of papers, magazines, books and other clutter is the first step. This way the puppy will not have anything to distract them. Getting rid of dirty dishes or food that are at a level the puppy can reach is very important as well. Young puppies especially will get into nearly anything if they can and that can be a problem for you. It's much easier for you to stop bad habits before they even start.

IN THE KITCHEN

This is one room of the house it may be difficult to keep your puppy out of but at the same time you want to make sure you're keeping the area clean so he doesn't get into things like the trash can or the food you have stored in the cupboard. You'll also want to keep the puppy away from things like electrical cords or chemicals. All of these things could easily be in your kitchen and if you're not careful they could become big problems for your new puppy (and for you).

Anything you would keep your young child away from you're also going to want to keep your new puppy away from as well. That means candles, glass ornaments or decorations and any type of medications. Your puppy will chew on anything even if they can't get into it and that could mean they end up with a mouthful of harmful glass when the ornament breaks.

THINGS TO KEEP IN MIND

Bones are another dangerous pastime for puppies. They could easily break if they are small and cause harm to your puppy. Make sure you only give your dog bones that are made for dogs and not the bones out of your chicken dinner or turkey.

Next are pins and needles. If you're a crafty person you know how easy it is to drop one of these and not be able to find it. A few days later you end up pricking your foot because you stepped on it. Well these are very dangerous for dogs because they can easily eat the needle and then become sick or even cut themselves inside their body.

Antifreeze is a huge problem. You definitely want to make sure it is kept far away from your dogs because it is extremely poisonous. Unfortunately it's also extremely attractive to dogs and if they find it they will drink it.

Pesticides and poisons are, by nature, poisonous. You want to keep them away from your dog as well. If you use them frequently them make sure you keep your dog away from any area that they are used or sprayed for at least as long as mentioned on the package.

Something you may not know is that plants such as poinsettia's, rhododendron, lily of the valley and fruit pits can be poisonous to your Aussie. These are extremely toxic even if they are generally safe to have in the home of humans. With a dog however, you have to worry about what they will put in their mouth and if it's any of these things (and select others as well) it could be fatal.

Think about what your dog is capable of when you puppy-proof. You need to know their size and their agility level extremely well in order to manage this. If you think something is out of your dog's reach then make sure you look again. Many dogs, especially these ones, are able to stand on their hind legs and may be able to reach items you thought were too tall.

Remember that anything in your house is potentially a jumping off point as well. Your puppy can easily jump up on the couch and then reach the shelves behind it even if you try and keep them down. They could also jump up onto a bed and get into the things in your nightstand. Remember all of the things that your dog is capable of when you start puppy-proofing your home, it isn't like a baby that will simply crawl around on the floor, your Aussie will be able to run, jump and more right from the start.

The Important Targets

It always seems like dogs are capable of finding the things that you really don't want them to find such as glasses, shoes, garbage cans, books, cell phones and remotes. They also tend to chew on these things rendering them completely useless. So make sure you're getting these things out of harm's way and keeping them that way at all times. You never want to leave a remote on the table where you dog can easily get it because they will. Always put things up out of the dog's way so they are safe and well protected.

Where to Start

The very first things you're going to need for your new puppy are bowls. You want to make sure you get both a food and water dish that are going to be big enough for a full grown dog. You'll be able to fill them up less in the beginning and then progress to giving your puppy more and more as it grows into adulthood. You'll also be able to save some money because you only have to buy the bowls once.

Of course now that you know what size to buy you still don't know which type. You can buy bowls made out of plastic, ceramic, stainless steel and more. Of course you're going to want to keep a couple things in mind when you select the right material and design. First remember that your puppy is strong and it's very possible that they will knock their bowl over at some point. So you're going to want a heavier bowl that is less likely to tip.

Another thing to keep in mind is that the bowl should not be able to crack. Cracks in the bowl cause bacteria to get inside of it which can cause harm to your dog. Make sure also that the bowl is not based with lead or painted with lead as some dog bowls still are and this substance is just as dangerous to your dog as it is to you.

SELECTING THE PROPER COLLAR

There are a variety of different collars available for any kind of dog and they come in all different sizes, colors, styles and more. Your best way to go about choosing a collar is to pick one that fits your puppy right now. Don't expect them to grow into it or keep it forever. Pick a lightweight collar that will simply get them used to the idea of wearing one. You don't need anything fancy or expensive. Just a simple latch collar will do. When they get too big for that collar then simply pick out a new one.

The size is easy to find though you may not think so. It's actually a very simple process. What you want to do is take a measuring tape and wrap it loosely around your dog's neck. Place two fingers between the tape and your dog and you'll have the right size for your needs. You may want to get something just slightly looser but you'll know what's best for your dog. Remember that you want to keep the collar loose enough that the dog can easily move and breathe even when running.

A buckle with higher safety features can be a good investment. Something that is too easy to open can often cause your dog to simply slip out of the collar or open it themselves even without meaning to. This can be a big problem which is why all the new latches were created. Talking with store personnel can be the best way to determine a good collar for your dog. Make sure you know what each feature is for and why it should be important before you spend your money on it.

You're also going to want to look at the prices of different collars. Some will be as cheap as five or six dollars while others could be close to a hundred. You'll be able to see which will fit your needs best. Remember it's not all about the price and you'll want to keep in mind the features the collar will provide when you're selecting one. Just because one collar is more expensive however does not mean that it's better quality.

Another aspect of collars to consider are reflective tapes. These can be applied to just about any collar or leash though some come with reflective tapes already on them. This is great when you're walking at night or in case (by unfortunate circumstance) your dog gets away from you at night. This allows other walkers or drivers to see your dog in case there is any type of problem.

Finally you'll want an ID for your new puppy. Traditional ID tags attach to the collar and provide your name and address or phone number in case your dog gets lost. Newer methods include microchips or tattoos which should be discussed with a vet before you choose them. These will help you locate your dog no matter where it ends up.

A microchip will allow your dog to be scanned and to transmit information back that tells who the dog belongs to. It's only the size of a single grain of sand so it won't hurt the dog in any way and it goes right under the skin so no one can easily get rid of it if your dog is ever stolen.

GET THE RIGHT LEASH

A leash doesn't require too much. You want something that is going to keep your dog safe. You want a 30 foot leash with an automatic reel rather than a chain leash. Your puppy will want to chew on the leash and a chain will be damaging to their teeth. So make sure that you are keeping your puppy on a proper leash. A short leash for walks could also be a good plan.

USE A GATE

Keeping your dog out of certain areas of the house can be very important. You want to make sure that you're getting baby gates for just that. This will help you protect your puppy from stairs or other dangerous areas of the house. Putting up these gates before you bring your new puppy over is generally the best option. You'll likely want to purchase one or two even if you don't have a plan for where to put them quite yet.

Special pet gates can also be found at pet stores or in special catalogues. These generally fasten in different ways and they also swing open easier. They are also taller than regular baby gates. This makes them better for your puppy who may be able to jump.

WATCH THE BED

You may want to purchase a bed for your pet. This can be more comfortable for them and will also be much better for you. On the other hand you'll likely notice that your bed is the place that your new puppy wants to be. You're going to want to convince your puppy to sleep in its own bed. The best way to do this is to purchase something soft, padded and comfortable. When the dog gets bigger you'll want to get them a bigger bed so they can get the support they need.

EXERCISE PENS

Typically an exercise pen would be an outdoor area where your Aussie can run and jump and play to his heart's content. This is an area where they are free to get their exercise however they want. Unfortunately these areas are typically not tied down and that means you will need to watch out for our dog getting over or under the pen. Make sure you remember however that this is not the way that your dog should get all of its exercise.

CRATING

It may seem cruel to put your puppy in a crate however this is actually a very common method used for training your dog. Crates keep your puppy out of trouble and they keep them safe as well. It's important that you don't put our puppy in its crate too much as it will want freedom to run and plenty of time socializing with you and the rest of your family but putting the puppy in a crate will help.

First you want to make sure that the crate you choose has no sharp edges that can hurt your puppy. You also want to make sure it's sturdy enough that you won't have to worry about your dog breaking through or tipping it over as this could hurt them as well. You'll also want to select a style and size that fits your dog. A secure latch can be instrumental as your dog will likely try and push their way out of the cage.

In order to get the right size crate however you're going to need to take measurements of your dog. You want something that is the size of your dog from the tip of its nose to the base of its tale. Of course this is only true for a fully grown dog. For a puppy take this measurement and add one foot so he has room to grow into the crate a little bit. Anything smaller can be dangerous and anything too big can be as well.

A large crate doesn't give your puppy the secure feeling they should have in their crate. They should have only a small amount of space to move around (though they should be able to move around easily). Anything to cavernous simply makes them feel lost. If you aren't entirely sure what size crate to get then let the person at the pet store know what type of dog you have. They should be able to direct you to the right crate.

PROPER GROOMING

You're going to need at least a few special tools for the very first time you start grooming your puppy. These tools are:

- Slicker brush
- Pin brush
- Shedding blade
- Canine dental products

If there are a lot of fleas and or ticks around your area you'll want a flea comb and some special flea medication as well to keep your dog from getting them in the first place. All of these things are easily found at any pet store and a pet store worker can help you to find them easily.

Another thing you'll want to get is a set of nail clippers. Your dog's nails should be trimmed at least twice a month so they aren't too long causing your dog problems. You can select either guillotine or scissor nail clippers. The important thing is just to make sure that you're not cutting their nails too short so either get a good book or resource or get a professional to do it.

Remember that the blade on your clippers needs to be sharp so you don't have any problems cutting your dog's nails to the right length. You'll also want to make sure you're not pinching your dog as this causes pain. If you choose to file your dog's nails after clipping you'll want to get an emery board that's intended for acrylic (fake) nails.

Grinding is another option rather than clipping your dog's nails however this requires a special touch and some skill. You'll want to get help from a vet or pet store worker for some assistance before you try this on your own. You wouldn't want to hurt your puppy.

BATH TIME

Baths are a very important part of taking care of your new puppy. You're going to need to get some shampoo and cream to give them a good bath and make sure all the products are intended for dogs. You want a mild shampoo for regular baths as these are formulated so your dog doesn't get dry skin. You may also want some cream rinse so that he doesn't get static especially if your house has low humidity.

BRING ON THE TOYS

Buying toys is the most fun. You'll want to get at least a few good toys that are hard or good for chewing as this will strengthen your dog's teeth and keep them from chewing on things you don't want them to like your furniture or shoes. You also want to make sure these toys are large enough that your dog won't be able to easily swallow any of the pieces which could cause them to get sick or even choke. If the toy isn't sturdy enough it's possible they could tear it apart and get the pieces as well.

Last of all you'll want toys that are easy to clean. You want to simply be able to toss it in a bucket with some water and cleaning solution and be done with it. You don't want to have to scrub at anything or spend a long time getting dirt or mud out of fabric.

So what should you get? Well you're going to want something rubbery rather than stuffed animals or rope toys. These can be very easily torn apart and can cause problems for your dog as they end up with small pieces in their stomach or caught in their throat. Bones can also be a problem as they break down and your dog could end up constipated. Finally avoid buying too many toys as this could be just as problematic as not having enough. All you're trying to do is keep your dog from chewing up things you don't want him to get ahold of.

The worst toys of all are plastic, wood or painted. Plastic toys are easy to crack and when they crack they tend to get small pieces all over that easily hurt your puppy or you if you happen to step on them. Wooden toys on the other hand can splinter which could cut your puppy or you if you happen to step on them.

Finally painted toys are a big problem because many dog products are still allowed to use lead based paints. You don't want your dog to chew on anything that has lead in it just like you wouldn't want your child to do so. That's why they recalled lead based paint after all. You'll want to make sure that anything you get for your puppy is not painted with these products.

CHAPTER 5- TRAINING OF ALL KINDS

Housebreaking your new puppy may just be the most difficult part of owning a dog. You're going to need to spend a lot of time and effort on this task and it's definitely going to be an ordeal. After all, your puppy is going to be harder to train than your child because it won't realize that going to the bathroom in the house is bad.

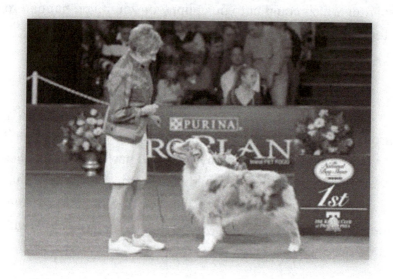

The first step in housebreaking is to understand your puppy's schedule. Look at when they have to go to the bathroom. Is it after they eat or after they sleep? Chances are if you watch them long enough you will see some type of pattern and you'll be able to take them outside before they end up doing their business in the house. If you take your puppy outside every time you even think they will go to the bathroom you'll be starting off the process very well. Until your puppy reaches approximately five months old they'll have difficulty controlling when they have to go to the bathroom and that means it's all up to you.

If you watch your puppy closely you'll likely notice that he tries to tell you when he has to go to the bathroom. He'll either move around restlessly or bother you incessantly. These are ways that your puppy says that he needs attention and wants to go outside. Take him out immediately rather than focusing on the nipping or the annoyance of him being underfoot. If you teach him not to do these things you'll never know when he needs to go.

WHERE HE GOES

If you're taking your puppy outside you want to know exactly where you want him to go. Find one specific spot and take him there. Give him attention or a treat when he reaches that spot and if he goes potty then you give him another treat. This reinforces the behavior that you're trying to achieve. Something to keep in mind when you're choosing a bathroom spot is that your dog is likely to be modest and want to go somewhere that will be away from others.

The first thing to really understand however is that our dog won't learn exactly the same way as other dogs. He may learn where to go to the bathroom after only a few tries whereas other dogs may take longer or your puppy may take longer to learn this technique. The important thing is to make sure that you're keeping up a steady routine just like when you potty trained your children. Practice consistency and every time your puppy (or you) does one of these things take them outside:

- Wakes up
- Eats breakfast
- Eats lunch
- Mid-afternoon
- Arrive home from work
- Eats dinner
- Before bed

If you can't come home in the middle of the day that doesn't have to be a problem. You can find a place where your dog can go to the bathroom such as a pad or paper and place it in a small, confined area. You want your dog to be trapped in this confined area where half of the space is taken up by the pad and the other half is taken up by their toys and food. They won't go to the bathroom where there stuff is and they'll learn the pad is the place to go. When you get home you'll want to take him outside immediately and then pay attention to taking him out anytime he has to go. The special spot is only for when you're gone.

ELIMINATE BARKING

Barking can be a big problem for any dog but you don't want them doing it for no reason at all. Your dog should only bark if something is wrong. The bark should be a warning of some type and not just a noise. After all, your neighbors aren't going to appreciate your dog barking at all hours of the day and night. But how are you going to make him stop?

If your dog barks then start by telling him to 'come.' This may seem like a strange command but what you're telling your dog is that you want him. If you want him then he focuses on you instead of on the barking and your dog isn't capable of easily doing both of these things at once. Of course the first thing you're going to need to do is teach your dog how to follow commands such as 'come' and others. This command especially can prove nearly invaluable to any dog owner.

MAKE A CALM PLACE

A calm environment will be the best place to teach your dog any new tricks or abilities that you want him to know. You want to make sure that wherever you train him is a safe surrounding as well and that it is as quiet as possible. Make sure your kids don't barge in while you're trying to train your dog since this can cause just as much trouble as a lot of noise. You need him to focus on you at all times rather than on distractions.

Once your dog is focused on you and is quiet you're ready to begin. You want to start by only moving a very short distance away and stating the command 'come,' you can even accompany it with a gesture if necessary to ensure your dog comes to you. Then give them a treat and reward them by petting or some other type of encouragement. You never want to punish your dog, simply don't provide the reward if he doesn't listen.

If you practice for ten to fifteen minutes at least twice a day you'll find that your dog is able to follow this command quicker than you would have thought possible. And make sure you're keeping his attention and having some fun with the training sessions or you could run the risk of not teaching him anything at all even though you spend a lot of time on it.

Repeat at the same distance for a long period of time and then make sure you move in small increments. Repeat the process for several days at one distance until you consistently get the reaction that you want. Make sure you're providing rewards such as treats each time your dog succeeds in the task you set for him. If you do give a treat make sure it's held directly in front of your face so they are forced to look at you when you hold it out to them. They will learn to always keep their attention on you at all times.

KEEP THE BARKING DOWN

If your friends or family come to visit the last thing that you or they want is a dog barking at them constantly. You want to teach your dog not to bark at people that he knows and not to bark excessively at any point in time. This requires some added work and a lot of effort on your part. You're going to need to understand the 'come' command and be willing to use it when other people are around. You can follow a special procedure to make sure that this happens properly.

As a 'guest' to knock on your door or walk by the house, whatever normally causes your dog to bark. Put your dog on his leash to reduce the risk that anything will happen and have a treat ready. When your dog starts to bark tell them to 'come' in a calm and firm voice. Your dog will turn and come to you and should stop barking when they do. Provide them with a treat as reward and repeat the procedure. You are not teaching your dog to never bark, you are simply teaching them to stop barking when you tell them to. You'll still get a warning when someone comes to the door but you won't have to put up with incessant barking that drives your guests crazy.

If something happens and your dog stops listening to you don't punish him. This will not help you and it definitely won't help him. Simply start your training again and wait until he learns what he needs to know. It may take a little time but you'll be able to get him back on track.

Separation Anxiety

Your kids likely had it when you dropped them off at daycare for the first time and maybe you did too but your dog likely has it as well. Put your puppy in a room and then walk out. Stay outside the room for a few minutes and then come back before your puppy starts barking. You want to make sure you're coming back before he barks so he knows that the barking is not being rewarded. You are rewarding his calmness at your leaving.

As he gets more used to being left alone for short periods of time gradually increase the length of time that you are gone. He'll get better and better at going long periods of time without feeling anxious because he knows that you will come back. You want your dog to be relaxed when you reenter the room which means that you may need to start by simply walking across the room and still being within sight. Only provide rewards if your dog does not bark and does not appear anxious.

CHECK YOUR ROUTINE

Think about what you do before you leave your house. You probably have a routine from the moment you get out of bed at the sound of your alarm until the moment you walk out the door. If you have a routine then you'll notice that your dog picks up on it. He will come to know that picking up the leash means it's time for a walk and after eating dinner it's time to go outside. He'll also know that when you pick up your keys you're leaving the house and leaving him behind. So make sure you aren't following too much of a set routine as this causes separation anxiety in your puppy.

Mix up your routine based on different days or different methods. You want your puppy to be confused about when you're going to leave the house so he doesn't get anxious before you even go. If you are ready to leave try leaving the TV on in one room of the house. You'll be amazed at how your dog gets distracted by the TV and doesn't even realize that you've left. There are a lot of different stations and many pet owners swear that the TV really does help their dog to feel better while they're gone. Not only is it bright and colorful but it's also full of new voices.

ELIMINATE CHEWING

Chewing on things can be a very big problem. If your dog is bored he will chew on things more than he would otherwise.

You definitely don't want that to happen because your dog will chew on anything and everything in the house. The first thing to do about this is to make sure that you are keeping anything important away from where your dog can reach so that it is in no danger of being chewed up when your puppy gets bored.

Dogs chew on things for several different reasons. These range from simply an innate desire to do so where the chewing is fun and rewarding to expelling emotions such as boredom or fear. We all know someone that eats when they're nervous or chews on their fingernails or has some other type of habit. Well your Australian Shepherd likes to chew as well. Finally your dog may chew simply to burn off excess energy because he's not getting enough exercise.

PREVENT CHEWING BEFORE IT STARTS

If your dog doesn't even get started chewing you'll have a better chance of keeping him from doing it in the future. You want to keep him from getting into things that shouldn't be chewed on and that means all versions of those things. You can't give your dog one old shoe to chew on and then expect that he won't get into the rest of them. You can't give him an old torn towel and think he'll know the difference between it and the new towels you just bought from the store. All of these things convince your dog that it's okay to chew and then they are confused when they get in trouble.

Your puppy will need something to chew on of course. Just like infants they need to strengthen their teeth and the best way to do that is with some type of chew toy. The important thing however is to make sure the chew toy is actually a toy and not something of yours that could become a problem later on. You can buy as many toys as you like but make sure you only give out a couple of toys at one time. Let your dog play with them for a short time before you put them away and bring out new ones. You can rotate the toys on a schedule and your dog will think there are tons of toys and never get bored with them.

SPEND PLENTY OF TIME

Another way to prevent chewing is to give your dog plenty of attention so he doesn't get bored. If he gets bored he's more likely to chew but if you're socializing with him constantly and taking him out of the house for exercise. If you catch your dog chewing it's important to never punish but to get his attention and take away the item he's been chewing on. Give him something appropriate instead and when he chews on that instead give praise. Your dog will learn that it's better to chew on the new item instead.

BE POSITIVE

The way you act toward your dog is going to have a huge impact on how they manage to succeed. You need to expect that your dog will get into some of your things and chew them up before you can save them. You also need to expect that it will take time and effort and a lot of patience on your part to convince your dog to stop chewing on things that he shouldn't. Simple take your time and help your dog to do what he needs and to chew only on the appropriate things in the house rather than all your treasured possessions.

CHAPTER 6- PROPER FEEDING AND NUTRITION

So now you have your own Australian Shepherd and your house is protected against any type of danger. You have plenty of toys and grooming and bathing supplies as well. You've also succeeded in housebreaking your puppy. You're ready to learn more about what your puppy needs to be eating in order to stay healthy and grow properly. You're going to need to learn a few important rules in order to do just that.

Your puppy is energetic and this type of dog will always be energetic so that means he needs food that is going to keep him happy and healthy while he continues to run around all day long. As a puppy he's going to need a lot of nutrients and a special food especially made for puppies. You want something that is going to be healthy for him and provide him with everything he needs to grow strong. The first thing however is to feed him exactly the same food and the same times that the breeder did. This will get him more used to you and cause less disruption in his life all at one time. Then you'll be ready to find the food you think is best.

Changing Foods

If you need to change the type of food your dog is eating you want to do it very slowly. Too rapid of a change could confuse him or even make him sick. You'll want to start with a mix of 25% new food and 75% old food so make sure you start this process when there's still plenty of the old food left. For several days you want to make sure you're following this process until your puppy is comfortable with the change and has no trouble eating his food. Next you'll switch to a 50/50 mix for a few days until he is comfortable again and then switch to a 25/75 split the other way before finally settling on 100% new branded food.

You want to make sure that your puppy has no health problems during or after the switch of food. He could have any number of difficulties and you want to make sure you're keeping an eye out so you notice them right away. Vomiting, loose stool or constipation are common problems that have been seen. You may need to spend more time on switching your puppy over or he could have a reaction of some kind to the new food.

Check Out the Options

Now there are plenty of different brands of dog food available out there. You're going to want to make sure you're checking out what each of them has to offer and doing your research to find out what's best for a dog of your breed, age, size, etc. You want to compare different types from dry kibble, semi-moist foods and moist foods. All of these will be slightly different though you'll want to look into certain traits amongst those different types of foods more closely.

The best option for an Aussie is typically dry food. Your dog may like eating the moist food however this contains a lot of water, sugar and salt which can cause health problems and generally doesn't provide the level of nutrients that your growing puppy needs. You're also getting a lot of water for your money which definitely won't help in filling up your puppy who will want to eat more and more.

FIGHTING THE BRAND

Before you go simply picking the cheapest type of dry kibble on the market you should know that not everything is the same. Even if you get a chicken kibble from one company and a chicken kibble from another they won't necessarily be the same thing. You'll want to look at the ingredients lists and determine what is going to be the best one. You want to make sure you're getting nutrients and healthy ingredients instead of just a lot of cheap filler ingredients. That's what a lot of economy priced brands provide.

Your puppy won't get the health benefits he needs from his food and could have all different types of health problems including improper growth or even unhealthy foods that cause him diseases or disorders that are more difficult to get rid of. Of course you won't necessarily have to buy the most expensive food since this is not necessarily any different from some of the moderate priced food. You'll be able to get something that has a high quality and a reasonable price if you're willing to shop around and check different places.

Higher quality brands are going to provide better quality ingredients. They may be similar ingredients but they'll be better versions such as fresher vegetables and meat. These are generally premium or performance brands which aid in digestion and even provide more nutrients per serving. If you don't know what to feed your dog then ask your vet. They will know the best choice for your breed of dog and your dog's individual health.

FEEDING FROM THE TABLE

Providing table scraps to your dog may seem like a nice treat but the truth is that it's anything but. You'll be tempted to give him something sweet or something special and he'll likely devour it like cake but that's a big problem for many different reasons not the least of which people food is unhealthy for dogs.

You've heard that a lot of the things you eat are unhealthy for you but they're actually 100 times worse for your dog. People food has a lot of additives and preservatives and ingredients that could not only be unhealthy but actually prove toxic to your pets. And once you get into the habit of providing table scraps you and your dog won't be able to stop. His balanced diet will go out the window and he'll likely end up with health problems and diarrhea.

WHEN IS FEEDING APPROPRIATE

Feeding your puppy is important of course but following a schedule is the best way to go about doing this. You'll want to find a way to fit feeding time for your dog in with your daily schedule so that you never forget or never put it off too long. If you leave the food in a bowl all day you're not going to be doing your dog any favors. Instead, you want to give him food three times a day and make sure there is no food at other times. During the day when he's older you can feed him a little more twice a day instead. This schedule will also improve your ability to predict bathroom times as well.

If your dog eats properly you should not let him run around much right after. You may want to have him rest or take him immediately outside as some dogs have to go to the bathroom right after eating. If he runs too much right away it can cause him internal problems and make him sick. So keep the kids away for at least an hour or two before letting everyone run and play.

WATCH THE FOOD

If your pet food tells you how much to feed your dog (and it probably will) you don't want to follow those directions immediately. You want to make sure you're feeding your puppy only as much as he needs and not overfeeding him. Often the instructions on the bag will be far more than your puppy actually needs and could end up with you making your puppy sick or your puppy getting overweight without either of you intending it.

The best bet is to start with small amounts of food and gradually increase the amounts as your dog turns out to still be hungry. You don't want to starve him but make sure that he's not simply eating more just because it's there (many dogs will). Only feed him until he's had what he needs for the time until his next feeding. You'll also want to make sure there's plenty of water available during and after all meals.

PROVIDING TREATS

Treats are great of course and your puppy is bound to love them but you want to make sure you aren't giving them too many treats. If you give your puppy over 10% of their calories in treats you're actually doing more harm than good. This is like eating junk food or candy instead of eating their regular dinner. It's something you definitely don't want them to do. So make sure you're giving out treats sparingly. During the early months you may want to stick to treats only during training so you don't end up giving out too many.

Hard treats can be the best option because they are not only a reward but also last longer than other treats. These are also great because they provide something for your puppy to chew on thus increasing the strength of their teeth and gums.

Understanding Water

Your puppy needs plenty of water in order to eat his food and he'll also need water frequently throughout the day. Think about how much you drink in an average day after all and your puppy is far more active than you are. Your dog needs a lot of water throughout any average day. If they exercise more than normal or the weather is hotter or anything changes they will likely need even more water throughout the day. So make sure the water dish never goes empty.

If your dog loses nearly all of its fat and half of its protein it can actually still survive but losing only 15% of the water in his body will kill him. That's definitely reason enough to keep water in the bowl at all times of the day and night.

WHY MIX DRY AND WET?

Feeding your dog dry kibble is the best option as we've already discussed. But why would you feed your dog so much dry food and then expect him to drink a lot of water to wash it down? Well that food is the healthiest option available and the reason for the water is just that, so he can wash down the dry, heavy food. Your dog needs a little help with his digestion especially as he gets older and the water helps to break down the food so it's easier to digest.

The water will also help to get rid of waste products through the kidneys and the rest of the body. Consuming water also has other benefits. It helps your dog get rid of bacteria and diseases and when you ensure the water you provide is always fresh and clear it helps with this as well. You're going to want to make sure the water in your dog's bowl is replaced frequently so that you don't inadvertently end up making him sick.

Still these aren't the only things you're going to need to keep in mind to keep your dog healthy. Grooming is actually an important step as well and it's actually the focus of the very next chapter.

CHAPTER 7- GROOMING TECHNIQUES

Getting this far means that you definitely take getting a new puppy very seriously. You're looking at getting a new dog as more than just gaining a pet, he's going to be a real member of your family. You're all ready with your house and training and you've figured out a lot of new things to help your puppy adapt to your family and your home. So let's get started with the next step in the process, proper grooming.

You could choose to consistently visit a groomer to take care of all of these needs however this could get very expensive.

It's also very time consuming to take your pet to the groomer every week (you should groom him quite frequently). You want to find a better way to do this and there definitely is one, groom him yourself. It's actually much simpler than you may think and that's why we have a whole chapter devoted to the best way to do it. You'll be able to give your new family member plenty of love and attention while he gets a nice pampering.

As we've already talked about it is important to clip your puppy's nails frequently but this isn't the only way you need to make sure you're taking care of them. You're also going to need to brush them properly to ensure that their coat stays clean and soft rather than getting dirty or matted which can easily happen during a normal day.

In order to properly brush your dog you're going to need a lot of the tools we talked about earlier. You're also going to need to keep in mind the fact that your dog has what's called a double-coat. This means he has a denser coat underneath the fluffy one on the outside that helps him to be protected. Keeping him well-brushed helps aid in that protection.

What you want to do is take only one small section at a time and start there. Brush from the skin all the way out to the ends of the fur. This uses what's known as a slicer brush which has curved bristles made of wire and a stainless steel rake. This appliance helps to brush both layers of your puppy's coat to keep him clean and neat.

Next you can use a tool to card out your puppy's fur which looks similar to a carding tool used with sheep wool. Make sure you're getting all the way to the bottom layer of fur as you brush and make sure you're checking for any problems the entire time. You'll also want to watch your dog to make sure he is enjoying the experience.

PROPER BATHING NEEDS

With many different breeds of dog it's important to bathe them ever week. With Aussie's however, this isn't the case at all. That's because there is a special oil that occurs naturally in an Aussie's fur so that they can keep themselves clean. This oil also keeps the dog waterproof so they are protected from any type of weather. This also means you can avoid bath time altogether in most cases and need only worry if your dog gets into something that he shouldn't be.

If you do need to bathe your dog then make sure you follow these steps. You'll want to get started with a few simple steps. The first of these is to put your dog in an empty tub and give them praise and treats. This tells them that it's a good thing to be in the tub. Next you'll want to keep him there until he relaxes and then allow him out and give another treat. You want to teach the dog to stay in the tub until you say it's time to get out.

You'll want to practice this at least once per day for several days before you try giving your dog a bath. Once he's comfortable just standing in the empty tub you can add a little water. You only want to get his feet wet so he understands the water is not a problem and there's nothing to be afraid of. Again you want to repeat this daily until he no longer has a problem staying in the tub until you feel it's time for him to get out again.

If you have a sprayer then the next step is even easier. Put him in the tub with a little water on the bottom and then wet him down all over. If he doesn't make any kind of fuss or try to escape then give him a treat. Repeat this process over and over each day until he has no trouble with being wet in the tub. At this point he's ready for a real bath and you'll be close to ready as well.

GETTING READY

Before you put water in the tub you want to make sure you're prepared fully for bath time. Just like with a small child you don't want to leave your dog in the bathtub and run off to grab something you forgot. Your dog likely won't drown but he will run away. So make sure you have everything you're going to need ready and waiting within arm's reach of the tub from the start:

- Dog shampoo
- Nonslip mat (for you)
- Towels
- Hose or container
- Cotton balls
- Eye ointment
- Brush
- Wash cloth

Each of these tools will prove important and each has its only step in the process. You'll start by brushing your dog down which can be done in or out of the tub. Make sure he's completely smooth and clean of any foreign materials. You'll next want to gently place the cotton balls in his ears so that he doesn't get any water in there which can be painful and dangerous as well.

Add ointment to his eyes just in case shampoo happens to get in. This can burn or cause other damage which you definitely don't want, especially the first time you give your puppy a real bath. It's now time to put them in the tub.

When you put the puppy in the tub make sure you reward him with praise. Then you'll wet him down with lukewarm water. Work the shampoo properly into his neck and down toward the tail, skipping over the face and head. You'll get to that later. You'll want to wash the belly, legs and under the tail before taking out a washcloth to gently wash his face.

WHAT ABOUT FLEAS?

If your puppy has fleas you're definitely going to want to get rid of them as soon as possible. It can be annoying but it happens to nearly everyone that has pets at some point or another. You can use regular dog shampoo to help get rid of fleas but other methods tend to work more effectively. There's actually a whole process for getting rid of fleas.

The first step is to make a collar around your dog's neck with suds and soap. Next you're going to lather up his entire body and instead of rinsing him off immediately you leave him soaped up for ten minutes. When you rinse him off there will be no more fleas because they'll be drowned out. Check his ears and head for fleas while you wait for the lather to work its way in and pull out any fleas with a flea comb.

Rinsing Off

Soap that clings to your dog for too long can cause problems in his skin. You definitely don't want that. So you want to make sure you're getting a thorough rinsing over his entire body. This is why it's easiest to use a hose attachment of some type to get all of the areas of your dog's body. When you've finished getting all the soap off you want to squeeze out any water from his fur with your hands and then pat him dry with a towel.

Don't worry if your dog races off to rub on things like carpet, furniture or walls. This is just part of his nature and it won't cause any trouble. You may want to take him outside as well so that he can go to the bathroom after sitting so long in the tub. You're not going to want to wait too long and you'll definitely want to make sure his collar is back on at this point in time.

Trimming Nails

Trimming toenails can be complicated at times but with the right technique it's much easier than you may have thought. You need to make sure you know what you're doing and that you prepare your dog for the task at hand before you even get started. Your puppy may even come to enjoy the nail clipping time (and bath time) if you manage to do it properly. You'll know it's time to trim again when you hear your puppy clicking across the floor whenever he walks.

PREPPING FOR NAIL TRIMMING

When you're just sitting on the couch or on the floor with your puppy play with his feet. Massage his toes or feet slowly so he gets used to you touching his paws. This will help him get used to the process that is going to occur when it's time to get started trimming his toenails for real. After he gets used to this you'll want to try trimming his nails for real. If he fights the first time then only trim one nail and praise him. The next day you'll want to try again and maybe you'll be able to get a little further before he fights it again. When you manage to get all of them in one session you'll both be very happy.

When you actually start trimming nails you want to make sure your puppy is comfortable wherever they are. Next you'll want to make sure you have the proper lighting. It doesn't matter how your puppy is sitting, laying or standing as you'll find a position that works for the both of you. Whether you want another person there with you to comfort your puppy or you put him on a leash and tie him up is completely up to you as well.

The first step however is to hold one paw firmly but not so hard that it hurts. You'll want to press on the pad of the foot to flex the nail. Next make sure you trim to just below the area where the nail trims down. There should be a black dot near the center of the nail known as the quick. If it's at the center then you've done good, if it's not then trim just a little bit further. Make sure you aren't trimming too far however. Trimming past the quick will cause pain to your puppy and it will bleed as well.

If you do trim a little too far (and it happens to even the best of us) you'll want to add styptic powder or cornstarch to the area right away. This will help to stop the bleeding and help your puppy feel better. Trimming nails should happen at least every three to six weeks but if your puppy's nails grow faster than this and you can hear him clicking across the floor it's definitely time to clip his nails again.

CHECK THE EARS

Your puppy's ears are very important. They should always be pink and they should always be clean as well. The ears are important for removing dirt from your puppy and that's a big reason that they need to be clean at all times. Do not use cotton swabs inside the deeper recesses of the ear as this can cause more problems than it solves. What you want to do is use a soft cloth and some ear solution. Hydrogen peroxide, alcohol, witch hazel and tea tree oil work well as substitutes for regular dog ear solutions.

Put a few drops of the solution into the section of the ear you're going to start with and gently rub the area until the wax loosens, then swab away with the cloth.

ON TO THE TEETH

The next step in keeping your puppy healthy and clean is to brush his teeth. Dogs can get gum disease and cavities just as easily as people can and that's why it's so important to check his teeth frequently. Make sure you're preventing these things as much as possible by taking good care of your dog's teeth from the start.

Once again you're going to need to follow a process to get your puppy ready for the first time you brush his teeth. You'll need to get started by touching his mouth and then touching his teeth with your fingers. Once these are considered common and he has no difficulty with them it's time to start out with the first teeth brushing lesson. You'll want to get some good meat flavored toothpaste from your local pet store and put a little on your finger. Put it in your dog's mouth and then slowly brush a few teeth at a time with the toothbrush.

Make sure you brush under the gum line and that you're doing a very thorough job. You need to brush in a circular fashion and try to do so as frequently as possible. It's best to brush your dog's teeth every day however this is generally not possible for the average pet owner. As a result it can be easier to use a scraper once or twice each month so that the plaque that does build up is scraped off.

Of course your dog likely won't appreciate the teeth brushing. They definitely won't appreciate teeth scraping. Still you're going to need to do these things and not rely on food or bones to keep plaque away. All of these grooming techniques are very important and all of them are going to be essential to keeping your puppy happy and healthy as well as looking good.

CHAPTER 8- HEALTH AND WELLNESS FOR YOUR PUPPY

Medical problems can easily arise for your puppy and that's why it's important that you follow all of the guidelines discussed above. You'll also want to be on the lookout for any type of health problems that may arise. Some of the most common of these are:

- Hip dysplasia
- Epilepsy
- Cataracts

Of course other health problems could occur but these will be the most common in this type of dog and are the ones that you'll need to look out for.

Hip Dysplasia

One of the most common and terrible diseases that could affect your dog is this one. It's a weakening of the hip caused by the ball and socket of the hip joint not aligning properly. If there isn't a perfect fit then tension occurs and ligaments start to have difficulty attaching. Your dog starts to suffer from pain and crippling that could become permanent.

In talking about this disorder your vet may discuss articular surface, the area of the bone where this specific ball and socket actually meet. This is a place of cartilage so that the bones don't rub together and cause friction. If the joint isn't quite right then there is a weakening of the muscles and ligaments. The articular surface disconnects and changes shape. It seems that this occurs over time and isn't a condition that the dog is born with as they are born completely healthy. It can lead to osteoarthritis.

SEEING HIP DYSPLASIA

This is not a trait seen only in older dogs and can actually be seen in dogs of all different ages. They may have trouble at as young an age as five months or may take on the traits as an old dog. There's no telling if or when it will occur in your dog. If it happens however there are several ways that you will be able to recognize the symptoms and take action before there is too much permanent damage.

If your puppy or dog seems to have difficulty walking or seems pained while walking take them to a vet immediately. The condition will not go away and will only continue to get worse and worse. You'll notice your dog is walking differently than before and that they are having more difficulty with running or jumping. They may have a stiff method of walking or have trouble walking up or down steps. All of these things are signs that your dog may be suffering from this disorder.

Nature Vs. Nurture

We've all heard the debate about what takes more of a toll on someone, their genetics or their environment. Well both of these things will have a role in whether or not hip dysplasia occurs in your dog. Genetics seems to be the biggest indicator however following a proper diet seems to have a great effect on keeping him from developing this disease in the first place even when genetics seems to point in its favor.

Obesity can be a worse precursor to the disease and cause increased severity. Too much growth during the first several months of life can also cause an increase in this disease. It's important, for this reason as well as others, not to allow your puppy to eat whatever and whenever they want.

Maintaining Diet

The diet of your dog needs to have a certain level of nutrients and calcium in order to keep him healthy and safe. Don't follow homemade meal plans such as giving your dog table scraps as this could negatively impact his ability to avoid this disorder and the problems that go along with it. This is not something that you are going to want for your puppy, that's for sure.

AUSTRALIAN SHEPHERDS AND EPILEPSY

Epilepsy is another problem that could be faced by our dog. This generally occurs between the age of two and three though it could happen as young as six months and as old as five years. This disorder seems very similar to the one experienced by humans and is evidenced by seizures of varying severity and frequency.

The cause of these seizures in dogs is not currently known 100%. There are several possibilities after all and that's what makes it important to pay close attention to everything about your dog. Congenital defects have been known to cause this problem as have extreme blood glucose levels. Anemia can also cause this problem as can all of the disorders or issues discussed below:

- Kidney disorders
- Liver problems
- Infections
- Brain tumor
- Toxins
- Brain damage
- Side effects of medications
- Fever

If you find that your dog has seizures or your dog is diagnosed with epilepsy you'll want to try and find out what is causing them and if there is another medical condition that needs to be taken care of right away.

Two different types of seizures exist which are grand mal and petit mal. A grand mal seizure is more common and far more dangerous. This causes convulsions, salivation and a feeling similar to temporary amnesia. Your dog will not recognize you or likely react to you in any way as they normally would. The petit mal seizure will likely cause a loss of consciousness. If your dog has multiple seizures at one time it can cause even more problems.

PHASES OF A SEIZURE

Seizures actually have specific phases which can be seen or discovered without your even realizing it. The pre-phase occurs when your dog knows something is wrong but isn't sure what it is. They may seem restless and pace or they may seek out your attention, hide, wine or anything else. Next comes the ictus phase where the seizure actually occurs.

In the ictus phase your puppy may vomit, salivate or run but they eventually will collapse and either begin convulsions or simply pass out. It is in the final phase that you will notice disorientation and possibly even temporary blindness all of which can last from a few minutes to several days.

Seizure Triggers

The cause of a seizure is technically unknown though some owners say that it occurs more frequently when the dog is excited or even sleeping. You want to make sure that if your dog is diagnosed with epilepsy you keep up with your vet regularly. If you think your dog may have epilepsy you'll definitely want to make sure you're getting them the treatment and help that they need as fast as possible.

Cataracts

The eyes of an Australian Shepherd have been known to be something special but unfortunately they are not as strong as one would hope. Many of these dogs develop cataracts which can only be cured or even treated with surgery. The clouding of the eye is the only symptom of cataracts in your dog, this occurs when the sodium water pump which keeps water and protein levels stable within your dog's eyes stops working properly.

Different types of cataracts are possible with some, such as congenital cataracts, being a genetic disorder. Another type are referred to as developmental or early onset. These occur early in life and may be inherited or caused by some type of outside trauma. It may even be something like an infection or diabetes in your dog that causes cataracts to occur.

Next are late-onset cataracts which generally occur in older dogs though it's far less common than the same type which occurs in humans. Finally is inherited vision cataracts. These occur as a result of the breeding that was done to produce the specific dog. It's very possible that this dog will pass on cataracts to any offspring that he may have.

Getting the right medical attention for cataracts is the best thing to do. There are plenty of surgery options that can help your dog continue to live a long and happy life without going blind.

CHAPTER 9- AUSTRALIAN SHEPHERDS

If you're looking for a show or competition dog then you're going to want to look into the American Kennel Club. You want to make sure you have all the information necessary to make sure your dog competes at the best level and that means getting the best dog and understanding what the AKC is really looking for when they judge those competitions. You're going to need to better understand the breed and the traits that it possesses from herding to loyalty and more.

LOYAL TO THE END

These dogs will protect you no matter what. They will be attentive and they will be excited at all times as well. The appearance of the dog is considered to be balanced where the length is nearly identical to the height. This dog is also considered to be of medium size and bone structure.

SIZING

This dog should be approximately 20-23 inches for a male and 18-21 inches for a female. It should also still have the medium size and bone structure as discussed above.

THE HEAD

Your dog's head should be proportionate to his body in size. It should have parallel plans at the back of the skull and muzzle and there should be a taper from the base of the nose. All of these things together make the Aussie appear as though it is intelligent and alert for anything that may come its way.

The Eyes, Ears and Teeth

The skull can be flat or domed and there is no true difference here. The eyes are possible to be blue, brown, amber, marbled or flecked according to the standards for breeding. With certain colorings of this dog it is even possible for them to be different colors altogether.

The ears of your dog should be triangular with moderate sizing and place high on top of the head. The ears should break forward and over or to the side if the dog is attentive or focused and should not hang down.

Finally the teeth should be strong, white and with a level bite. A couple broken teeth will not be a disqualifier however under or overshot teeth by more than 1/8 inch definitely can be.

Neck and Body

The neck should appear strong and sturdy as well as level and firm. The chest should be moderate and not to deep or too narrow. The ribs should also be considered "well sprung and long." The underline of the chest should be moderately tucked up and the shoulder blades should be long and flat.

The upper arms need to be similar in length to the shoulder blades and attach at a right angle.

The legs of course must be very strong with oval shaped bones. The pastern should be medium length. Dewclaws can be removed on the front however it is important that the feet are compact with arched toes and thick pads.

HINDQUARTERS

The width of the hindquarters should be equal to the width of the forequarters. There should also be a clearly defined knee with short hocks which are perpendicular to the ground and parallel to each other. Finally the rear dewclaws are required to be removed.

THE COAT

All hair on your Australian Shepherd must be medium texture and length. It is possible to have a straight or wavy coat with a reasonable undercoat as well. Hair on the head, ears, and front forelegs as well as below the hocks should be short and smooth. The back of the forelegs and 'britches' should show moderate feathering. Somewhat of a mane is permitted with a frill that is more present in male than female dogs.

COLORING IS EVERYTHING

The AKC has set several coat qualifiers which include blue merle, black, red merle, and red without markings which are all considered acceptable. There are also specific requirements if there is white on the neck of the dog as long as this is a full collar across the chest, legs and muzzle under. If there is a blaze on the forehead or an extension from under the body this is also acceptable though predominant white coloring is not considered acceptable.

WALKING TALL

The gait of your Australian Shepherd should be smooth and easy. He should walk well balanced and his legs should move straight, parallel to the center line of the body. When running the dog's legs should come almost all the way together with a firm, level back. The dog should also be able to change direction quickly and speed up or slow down just as fast.

Temperament can be of vital importance as well. This dog should be intelligent and should definitely experience a good-natured temperament. He should be slightly reserved though not overly so nor should he be considered aggressive or fearful.

CONCLUSION

Throughout the course of this book we've been able to introduce you to plenty of new concepts and ideas about your new puppy. You now know all about the Australian Shepherd breed and what you can expect from your new dog. You'll be able to check back with this book any time you need a little more advice and you'll definitely be able to find out plenty more information about your favorite dogs.

We've included a reference section as well as some other sources of further information about Australian Shepherds and other breeds of dogs as well. So take the time to look over some of our other resources and really get to know your dog better than ever before. You'll definitely be glad you did and your dog will thank you for it as well.

ABOUT THE AUTHOR

Hello, my name is Bowe Chaim Packer and I like to see myself as an open, *"**wear my heart out on my sleeve**"* kind of guy.

Some of the most important things to me in my life are:

- Laughing
- Kissing
- Holding hands
- Being playful
- Smiling
- Talking deeply with others
- Being loved
- Loving others
- Changing the world one person at a time (if my presence in your life doesn't make a difference then why am I here?) Hmmmmm, maybe that is a topic for another book. ;-)
- Learning from others (although often times I first resist). However, don't give up on me....
- Sharing ideas (no matter what they might be)
- Learning about others via most forms of contact.
- Traveling – hello, of course – almost forgot one of my favorite pass times.

Remember, LIFE is a journey for each and every one of us. We must never forget the things that are important to us or lose sight of what makes us happy.

CPSIA information can be obtained
at www.ICGtesting.com
Printed in the USA
LVHW082141041221
705306LV00013B/313

9 781633 831315